The Law of E. F. Hutton

John C. Maxwell

Participant's Guide

THE LAW OF E. F. HUTTON

Published by

A division of Thomas Nelson Publishers

Printed in the United States of America
ISBN 0-7852-9807X

For Information
Call Thomas Nelson Publishers 1-800-251-4000
www.thomasnelson.com

About the Author

Dr. John C. Maxwell, called America's expert on leadership, is the founder of The INJOY Group™, an organization dedicated to helping people maximize their personal and leadership potential. He is also founder of the nonprofit organization EQUIP™.

Each year Maxwell speaks in person to more than 250,000 people and influences the lives of more than one million people through seminars, books, and tapes. He is the author of more than 22 books, including, *Becoming a Person of Influence, The Success Journey, Developing the Leader Within You, Developing the Leaders Around You, The 21 Irrefutable Laws of Leadership,* and *Failing Forward.*

Introduction

As I travel and speak to organizations and individuals, people frequently ask me to define the essentials of leadership. "If you were to take everything you've learned about leadership over the years and boil it down into a short list," they ask, "what would it be?"

My book, *The 21 Irrefutable Laws of Leadership*, is my answer to that often-asked question. It has taken me a lifetime to learn these principles and I desire to communicate them to you as simply and clearly as possible. And it sure won't hurt if we have some fun along the way.

One of the most important truths I've learned over the years is this: Leadership is leadership, no matter where you go or what you do. Times change. Technology marches forward. Cultures vary from place to place. But the true principles of leadership are constant—whether you're looking at the citizens of ancient Greece, the Hebrews in the Old Testament, the armies of the last two hundred years, the rulers of modern Europe, the pastors in local churches, or the businesspeople of today's global economy. Leadership principles stand the test of time. They are irrefutable.

As we explore together **The Law of E. F. Hutton**, I'd like you to keep in mind four ideas:

- **The laws of leadership can be learned.** Some are easier to understand and apply than others, but every one of them can be acquired.

- **The laws can stand alone.** Each law complements all the others, but you don't need one in order to learn another.

- **The laws carry consequences.** Apply the laws, and people will follow you. Violate or ignore them, and you will not be able to lead others.

- **These laws are the foundation of leadership.** Once you learn the principles, you have to practice them and apply them to your life.

My desire is to see you succeed, and live life to your maximum potential by increasing your leadership ability. You can read my book and watch this video series in a few days, but it will take you a lifetime to maximize the laws in your own life.

Every session in this video course consists of three parts:

1. **"Case in Point" and opening discussion**
2. **Video Notes**
3. **Application and Assessment**

"Case in Point" contains a brief story that demonstrates the Law of Process in real life. Next, as you watch the video presentation, you will want to make a note of your impressions and personal reflections. Finally, the Application and Assessment section will take you more deeply into making this principle a part of your daily life, as well as assessing your current practices.

As you watch this video and work through these materials as a group, I encourage you to share your lives and learn from one another. All of us have experienced both success and failure as we grow in our ability to lead others.

Whether you are a follower who is just beginning to discover the impact of leadership or a natural leader who already has followers, you can become a better leader. The Law of Process—as well as all the other laws—is a tool ready to pick up and use to help you achieve your dreams and add value to other people.

Table of Contents

Session One 1
When the Real Leader Speaks, People Listen

Young, inexperienced leaders often walk confidently into a room full of people only to discover that they have totally misjudged the leadership dynamics of the situation. I know that's happened to me! But when it did, it usually didn't take me very long to recognize my blunder.

Session Two 13
Will the Real Leader Please Stand Up?

When it comes to identifying a real leader, the task can be much easier if you remember what you're looking for. Don't listen to the claims of the person professing to be the leader. Instead, watch the reactions of the people around him. The proof of leadership is found in the followers.

Session Three 25
Becoming the Real Leader

When most people think about Mother Teresa, they envision a frail little woman dedicated to serving the poorest of the poor. That she was. But she was also a real leader.

The Law of E. F. Hutton
Session One

When the Real Leader Speaks,
People Listen

Session One
When the Real Leader Speaks, People Listen

Case in point

Young, inexperienced leaders often walk confidently into a room full of people only to discover that they have totally misjudged the leadership dynamics of the situation. I know that's happened to me! But when it did, it usually didn't take me very long to recognize my blunder. That was the case when I presided over my very first board meeting as a young leader. It occurred in the first church I led in rural Indiana, right after I graduated from college at age twenty-two. I hadn't been at the church for much more than a month, and I was leading a group of people whose average age was about fifty. Most of the people in the meeting had been at that church longer than I'd been alive.

I went into the meeting with no preconceptions, no agenda—and no clue. I figured that I was the appointed leader and just assumed everyone would follow me because of that. With all the wisdom and knowledge of my two decades of life experience, I opened the meeting and asked whether anyone had an issue to discuss.

There was a brief pause as I looked around the table, and then a man in his sixties named Claude cleared his throat and said, "I've got something."

"Go right ahead, Claude," I said.

"Well," he said, "I've noticed lately that the piano seems to be out of tune when it's played in the service."

"You know, I've noticed the same thing," said one of the other board members.

"I make a motion that we spend the money to get a piano tuner to come out from Louisville and take care of it," said Claude.

"Hey, that's a great idea," everyone at the table started saying.

"I second the motion," said Benny, the board member sitting next to Claude.

"That's great," I said. "Does anybody else have anything?"

"Yep," said Claude, "I noticed the other day that there's a pane of glass in one of the Sunday school rooms that's busted. I've got a piece a glass out at the farm that would fit that. Benny, you're a pretty good glazer. How about you put that glass in."

"Sure, Claude," said Benny, "I'd be glad to."

"Good. There's one other thing," said Claude. "This year's picnic. I was thinking maybe this time we ought to have it down by the lake. I think it would be good for the kids."

"Oh, that would be perfect. What a good idea!" everyone started saying.

"Let's make it official," Benny said.

As everyone nodded agreement, we all waited to see if Claude had anything else to say.

"That's all I've got," said Claude. "Pastor, why don't you close us in prayer." And that's what I did. That was pretty much the whole content of my first board meeting. And it was also the day I realized who the real leader in that church was. I held the position, but Claude had the power. That's when I discovered the Law of E. F. Hutton.

Opening discussion/reflection:
What do you think might have happened if John had challenged Claude's leadership?

_____

_____

_____

_____

_____

_____

_____

_____

The Law of E. F. Hutton: *When the real leader speaks, people listen.*

_____
_____
_____
_____

Find the E. F. Huttons in _____ _____.

_____
_____
_____
_____

Ask the people in your organization the following questions:
1. Who would you go to if you wanted to get something _____?
2. Who would you go to if you wanted to _____ something?

_____
_____
_____
_____
_____
_____
_____
_____
_____

People watch the real leader for _____ when a decision needs to be made.

_____

_____

_____

_____

_____

You can tell who people consider the real leader by following their _____.

_____

_____

_____

_____

_____

_____

_____

_____

_____

_____

_____

_____

_____

_____

_____

_____

_____

Leading _____

> *If you see a disparity between who's leading the meeting and who's leading the people, then the person running the meeting is not the real leader.*

After my first board meeting, I had to determine how I was going to handle the situation in my first church. I had several options:

1. I could have insisted on my right to be in charge. I've seen a lot of positional leaders do that over the years. But that doesn't work. People might be polite to you, but they won't really follow.

2. Another option would have been to try to push Claude out as the leader. But how do you think that would have turned out? He was a member of that church before I got there, and everybody knew that he would be there long after I left.

3. I pursued a third option. About a week before the council met again, I called Claude and asked him if I could come out to the farm and spend some time with him. As we did chores together throughout the day, he and I talked about the long list of things that needed to be done at the church. He brought them up at the next council meeting and got everyone involved in getting these things done.

Have you ever been the positional leader of a group, rather than the real leader? If so, how did you relate to the real leader of the group?

_____

_____

_____

_____

_____

_____

_____

Knowing the Law of E. F. Hutton, would you do it differently now? Why or why not?

_____
_____
_____
_____
_____
_____

The _____ Have It!

Over the years, I have observed the Law of E. F. Hutton to be consistently true. I have sat through countless board meetings in which the one with the title was not in charge. In some meetings, the people were polite and respectful of the person with the title, all knowing however, who the real influencer was. In other meetings, I have witnessed outright disrespect and rebellion toward the official leader. In either extreme, or anywhere in the middle, the law still holds steady. People look and listen to the person with the most influence.

The next time you're in a meeting, see if you notice a difference between these two kinds of leaders:

POSITIONAL LEADER	REAL LEADER
■ *Speaks first*	■ *Speaks later*
■ *Needs the influence of the real leader to get things done*	■ *Needs only his own influence to get things done*
■ *Influences only the other positional leaders*	■ *Influences everyone in the room*

How would you rate your current leadership style on the continuum below?

Positional leader   **Real Leader**

1   2   3   4   5   6   7   8   9   10

From then on, if I wanted to accomplish anything at that church, I just went out to the farm and did chores with Claude.

7

I have never been the real leader at any job when I started it, other than at the companies I've founded. So, if you're starting in a new position and you're not the leader, don't let it bother you. The real test of leadership isn't where you start out. It's where you end up.

PERSONAL FACTORS CONTRIBUTING TO THE LAW OF E. F. HUTTON:

- Who you _____
- What you _____
- _____ you know
- What you have _____
- What you _____ are able to do

Personal Assessment

Consider the following questions to pinpoint areas for growth in living out the Law of E. F. Hutton.

BEFORE YOU SPEAK

1. **Do you have something of value to say?**
   ❑ Rarely   ❑ Usually   ❑ Always

   _____

   _____

   _____

   _____

   _____

2. **Have you done your homework?**
   ❑ Rarely   ❑ Usually   ❑ Always

   _____

   _____

   _____

   _____

   _____

3. Are you clearly aware of what you want to accomplish?
❑ Rarely ❑ Usually ❑ Always

_____
_____
_____
_____

WHEN YOU SPEAK

4. Do people listen?
❑ Rarely ❑ Usually ❑ Always

_____
_____
_____
_____

5. Who listens?

_____
_____
_____
_____

6. How long do people listen?

_____
_____
_____
_____

AFTER YOU SPEAK

7. Does anyone do what you ask or say?
❑ Few ❑ Some ❑ Most

_____
_____
_____
_____

Develop a solid relationship with the one who is the E. F. Hutton, help him or her succeed, and learn all you can. Your time will come!

8. **Do people ask you to speak more, or again?**
 ❑ Rarely   ❑ Usually   ❑ Always

_____
_____
_____
_____

9. **Do you more often regret what you said, or would you say it again, exactly the same way?**
 ❑ Usually regret   ❑ Usually approve

_____
_____
_____
_____

When others speak and you are present

10. **Do others in the group ask what you have to say?**
 ❑ Rarely   ❑ Usually   ❑ Always

_____
_____
_____
_____

11. **Do others look toward you and wait for comments before they speak?**
 ❑ Rarely   ❑ Usually   ❑ Always

_____
_____
_____
_____

12. **Do they look toward you or include your name (in a positive way) in their comments?**
 ❑ Rarely   ❑ Usually   ❑ Always

_____
_____
_____
_____

Closing discussion:

What is the most important thing you learned in this session? Why?

_____

_____

_____

_____

_____

_____

_____

Application and Assessment Notes

_____

_____

_____

_____

_____

_____

_____

_____

_____

_____

_____

_____

_____

The Law of E. F. Hutton
Session Two

Will the Real Leader Please Stand Up?

Session Two
Will the Real Leader Please Stand Up?

Case in Point

Many years ago, there was a game show called "To Tell the Truth." At the opening of the show, three contestants claimed to be the same person. One of them was telling the truth; the other two were actors. A panel of celebrity judges took turns asking the three people questions, and when time was up, each panelist guessed which person was the real truth-teller. Many times, the actors bluffed well enough to fool the panelists and the members of the audience.

When it comes to identifying a real leader, that task can be much easier if you remember what you're looking for. Don't listen to the claims of the person professing to be the leader. Instead, watch the reactions of the people around him. The proof of leadership is found in the followers.

Think about the reactions certain people get when they speak. When Alan Greenspan speaks before Congress, everybody listens. When he prepares to make a statement on lending rates, the entire financial community stops what it's doing. It's really a lot like the old E. F. Hutton commercials. When Martin Luther King, Jr., was alive, he got an incredible amount of respect. No matter where or when he spoke, people—black and white—listened. Today, Billy Graham gets a similar kind of respect because of his unquestionable integrity and lifetime of service. For nearly fifty years, world leaders have heeded his advice. Every president of the United States since Harry Truman has sought his leadership and wise counsel.

Opening discussion/reflection:
What are some of the common denominators of Allen Greenspan, Martin Luther King, Jr., and Billy Graham?

_____

_____

_____

_____

_____

_____

_____

_____

Video Notes

Positional leaders always declare their _____. If you have to tell people you're the leader, you're _____.

_____

_____

_____

_____

Positional leaders have a title, but not always a _____.

_____

_____

_____

_____

Real leaders have a following, but not always a _____.

_____

_____

_____

_____

_____

_____

_____

Positional leaders influence _____ people.

_____

_____

_____

_____

Real leaders influence _____.

_____

_____

_____

_____

_____

_____

_____

_____

_____

_____

_____

_____

Session Two
Application and Assessment

Influence is _____, not awarded.

The Law of E. F. Hutton reveals itself in just about every kind of situation. I read a story regarding former NBA player Larry Bird that illustrates it well. During the final seconds of an especially tense game, Boston Celtics coach K. C. Jones called a time-out. As he gathered the players together at courtside, he diagrammed a play, only to have Bird say, "Get the ball out to me and get everyone out of my way."

Jones responded, "I'm the coach, and I'll call the plays!" Then he turned to the other players and said, "Get the ball to Larry and get out of his way." It just shows that when the real leader speaks, people listen.

Why do you think the coach essentially allowed Larry to call the play?

_____

_____

_____

_____

_____

The Law of E. F. Hutton is a form of influence focusing on communication. This law is *not* about communication, but includes it. This law, like all laws on leadership is ultimately about influence — in this case, influence through communication.

_____are the message.

There is a wise proverb which states "It is not what you say, it is how you say it." There is much truth to that, but I will go one step further to add: "It is not what you say, but who says it!" Content certainly is important, but not as important as the one who delivers it.

In other words, the message is important, but the messenger is very important. You may have brilliant strategies, impressive degrees and titles, and a galactic-sized I.Q., but if people do not accept your influence, it is all for naught.

FIVE KEYS TO AN EFFECTIVE MESSAGE

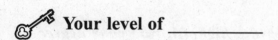 **Your level of _____**

Confidence comes largely from two sources, preparation, and experience. The more you prepare, and the more successful each experience is, the more confident you become. Without confidence, your influence will suffer, and people will not listen to what you have to say.

On a scale of 1-10 (10 being the highest), rate your confidence level:

1   2   3   4   5   6   7   8   9   10

_____

_____

_____

_____

_____

_____

_____

_____

_____

_____

Leadership doesn't develop in just a day. Neither does a person's recognition as a leader.

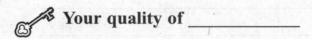 **Your degree of** _____

What you have accomplished sends a profound message about you as a leader. This area carries so much impact that if you are super accomplished in one field, people will listen to you speak, and want your opinion on anything, even if you know nothing about it!

Sports superstars are a great example. I recently saw a life-sized Michael Jordan cut-out photo advertising batteries in a local store. The quote was something like "Mike says they're the best." I will grant you that Mike may well be the greatest basketball player ever to wear high tops, but what does he know about batteries?! Nevertheless, people were lining up to buy them!

The point is that your accomplishments matter, and unless you are a super star, your accomplishments must be in the field that you desire to influence.

On a scale of 1-10 (10 being the highest), rate your degree of accomplishment:

1   2   3   4   5   6   7   8   9   10

_____

_____

_____

_____

_____

Your quality of _____

People do not always know what the issue is, but they can "feel" when something doesn't "seem right" about the leader. Blatant character flaws have the opposite effect that super competency does. You can be very accomplished, but your character can sell you down the river.

Go back in recent history in the sport of boxing. One of the greatest boxers, Mike Tyson, lost it all because of his character, not his skill and competency.

While your character is unlikely to have blatant flaws, I cannot emphasize enough the importance of integrity even in the little things.

On a scale of 1-10 (10 being the highest), rate the quality of your character:

1   2   3   4   5   6   7   8   9   10

_____

_____

_____

_____

_____

_____

⚷ Your measure of _____

Charisma is the ability to bring a sparkle into the room. It is the ability to create energy and cause people to feel good about themselves and the current experience. Charisma is light, hope, and joy. Charisma is faith, positive attitude, and confidence. Charisma is what draws people to you and makes the medicine go down easy.

Charisma is not magic. It is not possessed only by superstars, although they certainly have a greater portion than most! Charisma is not substantive, but it is significant. Leading without at least a modest level of charisma is an uphill hike.

The deeper the relationships, the stronger the potential for leadership.

The basics of charisma are relatively simple:
- Stay positive (no whining!),
- Encourage others,
- Smile,
- Remember and use names,
- Develop a good sense of humor (laugh easily and often),
- Believe the best about people,
- And most importantly, focus on others — not yourself.

On a scale of 1-10 (10 being the highest), rate your measure of charisma:

1   2   3   4   5   6   7   8   9   10

_____

_____

_____

_____

_____

Your quality of _____

Finally, we come to content. It is obviously important, but falls at the end of the list of priorities! Prepare thoroughly and prepare to the best of your ability. Speak wisely, at the right times, to the right people.

And remember the acid test: When you do talk, are people listening?!

On a scale of 1-10 (10 being the highest), rate the quality of your input to a specific group you are a part of:

1   2   3   4   5   6   7   8   9   10

_____

_____

_____

_____

_____

Closing discussion:

Which of the five keys discussed above presents the greatest challenge to you? Why?

_____

_____

_____

_____

_____

_____

_____

_____

Application and Assessment Notes

_____

_____

_____

_____

_____

_____

_____

_____

_____

_____

_____

_____

_____

_____

The Law of E. F. Hutton
Session Three

Becoming the Real Leader

Session Three
Becoming the Real Leader

Case in Point

I read something about Mother Teresa. When most people think about her, they envision a frail little woman dedicated to serving the poorest of the poor. That she was. But she was also a real leader. Lucinda Vardey, who worked with Mother Teresa on the book *The Simple Path*, described the nun as "the quintessential, energetic entrepreneur, who has perceived a need and done something about it, built an organization against all odds, formulated its constitution, and sent out branches all over the world."

The organization Mother Teresa founded and led is called the Missionaries of Charity. While other vocational orders in the Catholic Church declined, hers grew rapidly, reaching more than four thousand members during her lifetime (not including numerous volunteers). Under her direction, her followers served in twenty-five countries on five continents. In Calcutta alone, she established a children's home, a center for people with leprosy, a home for people who were dying and destitute, and a home for people suffering with tuberculosis or mental disorders. Only a true leader can accomplish that kind of organizational building.

Author and former presidential speechwriter Peggy Noonan wrote about a speech Mother Teresa gave at the National Prayer Breakfast in 1994:

"The Washington establishment was there, plus a few thousand born-again Christians, orthodox Catholics, and Jews. Mother Teresa spoke of God, of love, of families. She said we must love one another and care for one another. There were great purrs of agreement.

"But she became more direct as she continued to speak. She spoke of unhappy parents in old people's homes who are 'hurt because they are forgotten.' She asked, 'Are we willing to give until it hurts in order to be with our families, or do we put our own interests first?'

"The baby boomers in the audience began to shift in their seats. And she continued. 'I feel that the greatest destroyer of peace today is abortion,' she said, and told them why, in uncompromising terms. For about 1.3 seconds there was silence, then applause swept the room. But not everyone clapped; the President and First Lady, the Vice President and Mrs. Gore looked like seated statues at Madame Tussaud's, moving not a muscle. Mother Teresa didn't stop there either. When she was finished, there was almost no one she hadn't offended!"[1]

If just about any other person in the world had made those statements, people's reactions would have been openly hostile. They would have booed, jeered, or stormed out. But the speaker was Mother Teresa. She was probably the most respected person on the planet at that time. So, everyone listened to what she had to say, even though many of them violently disagreed with it. In fact, every time that Mother Teresa spoke, people listened. Why? She was a real leader, and when the real leader speaks, people listen.

Opening discussion/reflection:
What are some of the qualities that make Mother Teresa such a challenging model of leadership?

_____

_____

_____

[1] Peggy Noonan, *Time* 15 September 1997.

Video Notes

Real Leaders become Real Leaders because of _____.
 (Who they are)

_____

_____

_____

Real Leaders become Real Leaders because of _____.
 (Who they know)

_____

_____

_____

Real Leaders become Real Leaders because of _____.
 (What they know)

_____

_____

_____

Real Leaders become Real Leaders because of _____.
 (What they feel)

_____

_____

_____

Real Leaders become Real Leaders because of _____ .
   (Where they've been)

_____

_____

_____

Real Leaders become Real Leaders because of _____ _____ .
   (What they've done)

_____

_____

_____

_____

Real Leaders become Real Leaders because of _____ .
   (What they can do)

_____

_____

_____

_____

_____

_____

_____

_____

> *Knowledge alone won't make someone a leader, but without it, he can't become one.*

_____ Leaders Because . . .

How do the real leaders *become* the real leaders within groups? Just as leadership does not develop in a day, neither does a person's recognition as a leader. Over the course of time, seven key areas reveal themselves in leader's lives that cause them to step forward as leaders:

1. **CHARACTER—WHO THEY ARE**
   True leadership always begins with the inner person.

2. **RELATIONSHIPS—WHO THEY KNOW**
   The deeper the relationships, the stronger the potential for leadership.

3. **KNOWLEDGE—WHAT THEY KNOW**
   You need a grasp of the facts, an understanding of the factors involved, and a vision for the future.

4. **INTUITION—WHAT THEY FEEL**
   Leadership demands an ability to deal with numerous intangibles.

5. **EXPERIENCE—WHERE THEY'VE BEEN**
   Experience doesn't guarantee credibility, but it encourages people to give you a chance to prove that you are capable.

6. **PAST SUCCESS—WHAT THEY'VE DONE**
   Nothing speaks to followers like a good track record.

7. **ABILITY—WHAT THEY CAN DO**
   The bottom line for followers is a leader's capability. If they no longer believe you can deliver, they will stop listening.

Communicate, Communicate, _____

Silence is golden, wait your turn, but remember: leaders communicate. They know when to speak, and have a valuable contribution to make. You cannot lead if you do not speak. The saying: "He is a man of few words" is more often ascribed to a philosopher type, not an effective leader.

Leaders must be with people, and when you are with people, you must communicate to influence. (Your example does communicate as well, but the point here is the necessity of verbal expression in order to influence.)

Listen long enough to hear others' thoughts and opinions, listen to be courteous and respectful, listen to learn, and then speak to benefit others by your contribution.

Leaders strive to add value and move the mission or project forward.

Do you tend to say little or much at meetings?
❑ **Too little**   ❑ **Too much**   ❑ **Balanced input**

How can you determine if your input adds value?

_____

_____

_____

_____

_____

_____

MASTER THE ART OF 30 SECOND COMMUNICATION

Study the million-dollar Super Bowl commercials. They will give you an excellent idea of how to communicate both thoroughly and concisely.

Experience doesn't guarantee credibility, but it encourages people to give you a chance to prove that you are capable to lead.

> *Each time I enter a new leadership position, I immediately start building relationships. Build enough of the right kinds of relationships with the right people, and you can become the real leader in an organization.*

Remember, the law of E. F. Hutton is not about communication, but it does include it. *The point is leadership, the vehicle is communication.*

People do not tolerate long-winded, pointless communication. They will turn you off quickly, even if you had a good point to make. Know what you want to say, who you want to hear it, and the results you desire . . . before you speak.

SIX STEPS TO BECOMING AN E. F. HUTTON

1. ☐ Listen
2. ☐ Look
3. ☐ Lead
4. ☐ Look
5. ☐ Learn
6. ☐ Lead

Place a check next to each step above that you already do on a regular basis (in the proper sequence).

Why is the order of these steps important?

_____

_____

_____

_____

_____

_____

If things are not going the way you would like them to, perhaps someone else has garnered more influence than you. Do not fight the tide. Swim with the current until you have earned the favor of influence.

In other words, if you clearly are not yet the E. F. Hutton you would like to be, take the time to invest in your personal growth so others will want to listen to you. Develop a solid relationship with the one who is the E. F. Hutton, help him or her succeed, and learn all you can. Your time will come!

_____ you get in hot water . . .

Leadership is an artful endeavor — it is constantly fluid and keeps you on your toes. A mental nap at the wrong time can be lethal. On occasion, no matter how experienced a leader you are you will find yourself in hot water.

Let me offer you some insights to get you back on track.

- 👎 **Do not** be defensive.
- 👎 **Do not** assert your formal training and qualifications.
- 👎 **Do not** hold a grudge against anyone.
- 👍 **Do** admit you have made a mistake(s).
- 👍 **Do** take responsibility, no matter what you have done.
- 👍 **Do** give others the benefit of the doubt.
- 👍 **Learn** from your mistakes.
- 👍 **Get on with your life!**

Have you ever found yourself (or someone you know) in "hot water" as a leader? Describe.

_____
_____
_____
_____
_____
_____

How many of the above tips did you engage in getting yourself out?

_____
_____
_____
_____
_____
_____

How do people react when you communicate? When you speak, do people listen—I mean really listen? Or do they wait to hear what someone else has to say before they act?

Action Assignment

Observe others carefully when you are up to bat—whether speaking in a meeting, delivering a sermon, giving a sales presentation, debating an issue or talking to your kids! Are people listening? Are they responding as you desire? Are you making significant changes because of your influence?

The encouraging thing for all leaders is that you can increase your influence. The practical insights you have learned in this video course will help you do just that.

1. **List the top three areas where you influence people** *(from the seven areas listed at the beginning of this session).*

   _____

   _____

   _____

2. **List the top three areas where other influencers that you know influence people.**

   Name   **Area of influence**

   _____   _____

   _____   _____

   _____   _____

3. **Make it a practice to speak out and lead in your three areas of strength.**

4. **Support and learn from the strengths of the other influencers you listed.**

Closing discussion:

Name one leader—either widely known or a personal acquaintance—whom you believe best demonstrates the Law of E. F. Hutton. Explain your answer.

_____

_____

_____

_____

_____

_____

_____

Application and Assessment Notes

_____

_____

_____

_____

_____

_____

_____

_____

_____

_____

_____

_____

_____

OTHER EZ LESSON PLANS

The EZ Lesson Plan was designed with the facilitator in mind. This new format gives you the flexibility as a teacher to use the video as the visual and then refer to the facilitator's guide for the questions ... and even better, the answers. It is designed for a four-week study, communicated by our top authors and it is totally self contained. **Each EZ Lesson Plan requires the student's guides to be purchased separately as we have maintained a very low purchase price on the video resource.**

Please visit your local Christian bookstore to see the other titles we have available in the EZ Lesson Plan format. We have listed some of the titles and authors for your convenience:

The 10 Commandments of Dating   Ben Young and Dr. Samuel Adams

Are you tired of pouring time, energy, and money into relationships that start off great, and end with heartache? If so, you need "The 10 Commandments of Dating" to give you the hard-hitting, black-and-white, practical guidelines that will address your questions and frustrations about dating. This guide will help you keep your head in the search for the desire of your heart.

EZ Lesson Plan ISBN: 0-7852-9619-0   **Student's Guide ISBN: 0-7852-9621-2**

Extreme Evil: Kids Killing Kids   Bob Larson

Kids are killing kids in public schools! Kids are killing their parents! What is causing all of this evil in our younger generation? Do we need prayer back in the schools ... or do we need God to start in the home? Bob Larson gets us to the root of these evils and brings us some of the answers we are looking for in this new video assisted program.

EZ Lesson Plan ISBN: 0-7852-9701-4   **Student's Guide ISBN: 0-7852-9702-2**

Life Is Tough, but God Is Faithful   Sheila Walsh

Sheila takes a look at eight crucial turning points that can help you rediscover God's love and forgiveness. Showing how the choices you make affect your life, she offers insights from the book of Job, from her own life, and from the lives of people whose simple but determined faith helped them become shining lights in a dark world.

EZ Lesson Plan ISBN: 0-7852-9618-2   **Student's Guide ISBN: 0-7852-9620-4**

Why I Believe   D. James Kennedy

In this video, Dr. D. James Kennedy offers intelligent, informed responses to frequently heard objections to the Christian faith. By dealing with topics such as the Bible, Creation, the Resurrection, and the return of Christ, "Why I Believe" provides a solid foundation for Christians to clarify their own thinking while becoming more articulate in the defense of their faith.

EZ Lesson Plan ISBN: 0-7852-8770-9   **Student's Guide ISBN: 0-7852-8769-5**

The Lord's Prayer   Jack Hayford

Why do we say "Thy Kingdom come?" What does "Hallowed be Thy Name" mean? Do we really practice "Forgive us our debts as we forgive our debtors?" Pastor Jack Hayford walks you through verse by verse and then applies this great scripture to our personal lives. This study will put "meaning to the words" you have just been saying for years.

EZ Lesson Plan ISBN: 0-7852-9442-2   **Student's Guide ISBN: 0-7852-9609-3**

How To Pray

Ronnie Floyd

Whether you are a rookie in prayer or a seasoned prayer warrior, this video kit will meet you where you are and take you to another level in your prayer life. You may have been raised in a Christian home where prayer was a normal, daily exercise. You may have attended church all of your life, where the prayers of the people and the minister were as common as the hymns that still ring in your ears. Yet such experiences do not guarantee that you know how to pray. With simple, yet profound prose, Dr. Floyd declares, "prayer occurs when you depend on God, prayerlessness occurs when you depend on yourself."

EZ Lesson Plan ISBN: 0-8499-8790-3   **Student's Guide ISBN: 0-8499-8793-8**

Jesus and The Terminator

Jack Hayford

From the **E-Quake** Series comes the EZ Lesson Plan that is the focal point of the Book of Revelation. Pastor Hayford sets the stage for the fight against the Evil One when the end of time comes upon us. There is no greater force than that of Jesus, and now viewers will see Him become triumphant again in this battle that is evident.

EZ Lesson Plan ISBN: 0-7852-9601-8   **Student's Guide ISBN: 0-7852-9658-1**

The Law of Process

John C. Maxwell

Leadership develops daily, not in a day. This law, taken from **The Twenty One Irrefutable Laws of Leadership** is the first of the series to be placed into an individual study. Take each opportunity as it comes along and find the answer in a way only strong leaders would do it … by processing it. John explains how and why "Champions don't become champions in the ring … they are merely recognized there."

EZ Lesson Plan ISBN: 0-7852-9671-9   **Student's Guide ISBN: 0-7852-9672-7**

Forgiveness

John MacArthur

In this three-session EZ Lesson Plan, noted biblical scholar John MacArthur provides an insightful look at forgiveness. MacArthur not only reminds us that we are called to grant forgiveness to those who sin against us, but he also teaches the importance of learning to accept the forgiveness of others.

EZ Lesson Plan ISBN: 0-8499-8808-X   **Student's Guide ISBN: 0-8499-8809-8**

Healing Prayer

Reginald Cherry, M.D.

"Prayer is the divine key that unlocks God's pathway to healing in both the natural and supernatural realms of life." In "Healing Prayer," Dr. Cherry explores the connection between faith and healing, the Bible and medicine. Cherry blends the latest research, true stories, and biblical principles to show that spirit-directed prayers can bring healing for disease.

EZ Lesson Plan ISBN: 0-7852-9666-2   **Student's Guide ISBN: 0-7852-9667-0**

The Andy Griffith Show Bible Study Series – Vol. II

Systems Media, Inc.

For generations, stories have been used to teach universal truths. In keeping with this time-honored tradition, the new four-volume Andy Griffith Bible Study Series uses the classic stories of Mayberry to illustrate biblical truths. Learn from Andy, Opie, and the gang as they struggle with, and learn from, everyday life situations.

EZ Lesson Plan ISBN: 0-8499-8815-2   **Student's Guide ISBN: 0-8499-8816-0**

Becoming A Woman of Grace

Cynthia Heald

This is a newly formatted product built around a message that only Cynthia Heald could deliver to us. Women have proven to be the stronger of the sexes in prayer, empathy and faith. Cynthia leads this women's group study on how a woman can become A Woman of Grace through prayer, obedience to God, and other practices of her life. This EZ Lesson Plan will bring the components of this publishing product to one, self-contained format ready to start small groups.

EZ Lesson Plan ISBN: 0-7852-9706-5   **Student's Guide ISBN: 0-7852-9707-3**

Created To Be God's Friend

Henry Blackaby

Henry Blackaby, being born a man of God, living his life as a man of God, teaches us how all of us are created equal in being God's friend. No Christian need live without a keen sense of purpose, and no believer need give up on finding daily closeness with God.

EZ Lesson Plan ISBN: 0-7852-9718-9   **Student's Guide ISBN: 0-7852-9719-7**

Resurrection

Hank Hanegraaff

In this definitive work, popular Christian apologist Hank Hanegraaff offers a detailed defense of the Resurrection, the singularly most important event in history and the foundation upon which Christianity is built. Using the acronym F.E.A.T., the author examines the four distinctive, factual evidences of Christ's resurrection—Fatal torment, Empty tomb, Appearances, and Transformation—making the case for each in a memorable way that believers can readily use in their own defense of the faith.

EZ Lesson Plan ISBN: 0-8499-8798-9   **Student's Guide ISBN: 0-8499-8799-7**

The Murder of Jesus

John MacArthur

To many, the story of Christ's crucifixion has become so familiar that it has lost its ability to shock, outrage or stir any great emotion. In "The Murder of Jesus," John MacArthur presents this moment in the life of Jesus in a way that forces the viewers to witness this event in all its power. The passion of Christ is examined chronologically through the lens of the New Testament with special attention to Jesus' words on the cross, the miracles attending the crucifixion, and Christ's atoning work.

EZ Lesson Plan ISBN: 0-8499-8796-2   **Student's Guide ISBN: 0-8499-8797-0**

Fresh-Brewed Life

Nicole Johnson

God is calling us to wake up, to shout an enthusiastic "Yes" to life, just as we say "Yes" to our first cup of coffee each morning. Nothing would please Him more than for us to live fresh-brewed lives steeped with His love, filling the world with the marvelous aroma of Christ. The EZ Lesson Plan will provide humor, vignettes, and in-depth study to small groups all over on this topic.

EZ Lesson Plan ISBN: 0-7852-9723-5   **Student's Guide ISBN: 0-7852-9724-3**

The Law of Respect

John C. Maxwell

Our parents teach us to respect others. Our business practices are to be ones of respecting others, ideas, thoughts, and mainly their motivations. We tend to get caught up in the daily routines, but if we do not respect those around us and the ones we work with, our success will be held at a low ebb. John Maxwell is a leader's leader.

EZ Lesson Plan ISBN: 0-7852-9756-1   **Student's Guide ISBN: 0-7852-9757-X**

The Ten Commandments

Jack Hayford

We are all taught the Ten Commandments early in our Christian walk. Dr. Jack Hayford now takes us one step farther and teaches us each of these commandments by a video-assisted method. Dr. Hayford teaches us to honor our fathers and our mothers by first teaching us to honor our Lord. All ten commandments will be taught over a four-session study. Studies with the comprehensive study material sold separately.

EZ Lesson Plan ISBN: 0-7852-9771-5　　　　　　　　　　**Student's Guide ISBN: 0-7852-9772-3**

Fit To Be a Lady

Kim Camp

Kim Camp shows moms how to make it through the difficult years of parenting pre-adolescent daughters by nurturing their girls in the love and grace of God—the source of all self-worth and confidence. Camp examines such topics as peer influences, music and the media, sex and purity, and diet and exercise.

EZ Lesson Plan ISBN: 0-8499-8827-6　　　　　　　　　　**Student's Guide ISBN: 0-8499-8828-4**